Kateri Tekakwitha

THE FIRST ABORIGINAL WOMAN SAINT WHO DIED "BEAUTIFUL" | CANADIAN HISTORY FOR KIDS

True Canadian Heroes – Indigenous People of Canada Edition

www.ProfessorBeaver.ca

Print Edition: 9780228235408
Digital Edition: 9780228235415
Hardcover Edition: 9780228235934

Published by Speedy Publishing Canada Limited

PROFESSOR
BEAVER
Building Smarter and Brighter Minds

Table of Contents

Quick Facts

Kateri Tekakwitha lived many years ago, in the 1600s. She was a member of an Indigenous (a person who was the first to live in a certain area) group of people. Her father was a Chief (leader) of the Mohawk People and her mother was a Roman Catholic Algonquin.

Did you know?

The Mohawk people are from the Iroquoian people, an Indigenous group from North America. They used to live in the eastern part of the state of New York in the United States of America (USA). The Algonquin people are an Indigenous people who come from areas around the Ottawa River and the area near Lake Superior in Canada.

Kateri Tekakwitha

Kateri became an orphan when she was four years old.

Kateri's full name, Kateri Tekakwitha, is pronounced ['gaderidega'gwita] in the Mohawk language.

Kateri became an orphan (a child whose parents have died) when she was four years of age.

She was the first Indigenous person from North American who became a Roman Catholic saint (a person who is believed to have lived an extremely good life on Earth and who is now in heaven).

Kateri died in 1680. She left a legacy (things that are left behind after a person has died) and she has become a legend (a traditional story that has been handed down from one generation of people to another).

Stained glass window of St. Kateri Tekakwitha, known as Lily of the Mohawks, a Native American saint canonized in 2012 and patron of the environment and ecology

Kateri's Birth and Early Years

Kateri was born in 1656 in Ossernenon which is now called Auriesville in the state of New York. Her father's name was Kenneronkwa Tekakwitha and her mother's name was Tagaskouita Tekakwitha. Kateri had one brother and he was younger than she was.

NEW YORK

SSERNENON

R MOHAWK INDIAN
TLE 1642-1659.
JOGUES AND RENE
MARTYRED HERE.
WITHA BORN HERE

STATE EDUCATION
DEPARTMENT 1932

Ossernenon
Historical Marker

When Kateri was four years old, the village in which she lived had a smallpox epidemic.

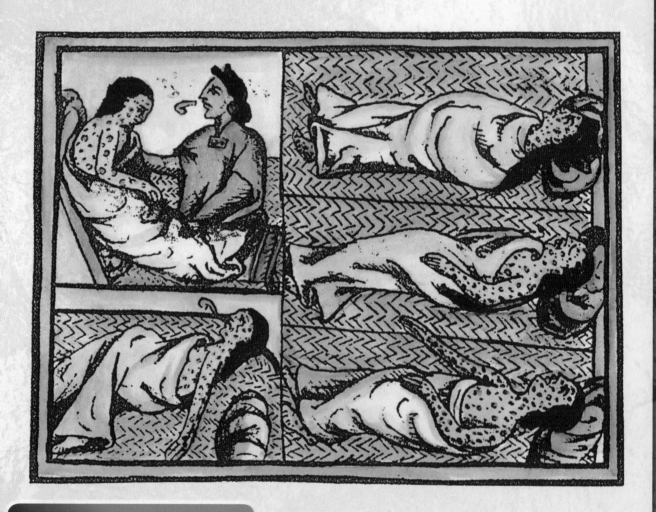

Smallpox is a very bad contagious disease.

Did you know?

Smallpox is a contagious (can be passed from one person to another) disease. It used to be common but because of vaccinations (something a person can be given that prevents the body from getting a certain disease) it is no longer a disease which people can get naturally. An epidemic is when many people in a certain area get a disease at the same time.

Kateri, her parents, and her younger brother caught smallpox. Kateri was the only person in her family who did not die from the disease. However, smallpox left her with many scars on her body and very bad eyesight. After her parents and brother died, Kateri went to live with her uncle and other relatives.

In 1666, when Kateri was ten years old, Ossernenon, the village in which she lived, was destroyed by the French. (The French had come to North America from France in Europe). Because the village was destroyed, Kateri and her relatives had to relocate (move). They went across the Mohawk River or Rivière des Hollandais, as it is also known, and built a new village by the name of Gandaouagué.

The Mohawk River winds through Mohawk Valley near Little Falls, New York.

Saint Ignatius of Loyola

AD
MAIOREM
GLORIAM
QVICVNQVE H
IESV CHRISI
TIÆ NOMEN
DERINT, DIE N
TEQVE SVCCI
TI LVMBOS ET
TAM GRANDIS
BITI SOLVTIONEM
MPTI ESSE EBER

After Kateri and her relatives had been living in Gandaouagué for a year, three Jesuit missionaries came.

Did you know?

Jesuits are an order (group) of clergy from the Roman Catholic Church. The order was founded (started)in 1534 by Saint Ignatius of Loyola. Jesuit missionaries are clergy who go to different places to teach people about Christianity.

The three Jesuit missionaries who came to Gandaouagué established (set up) the St. Pierre Mission, a place that was a Church and a place that helped people.

Kateri Joins the Roman Catholic Church

*K*ateri took an interest in the Jesuit missionaries and their teachings. She was a good friend of Father Jacques de Lamberville who was the head of the St. Pierre Mission. She told him that she wanted to become Roman Catholic. Therefore, Father de Lamberville taught the Catechism (the teachings of the Roman Catholic Church) to Kateri.

Father Jacques de Lamberville taught the Catechism to Kateri.

Baptism is the sacrament in which people join the Roman Catholic Church.

When Kateri was twenty years of age, she became baptized into the Roman Catholic Church. Her baptism occurred during the period of Easter in 1676. The actual date was April 18th, 1676.

Did you know?

To Roman Catholics, Baptism is the sacrament (Christian practice) in which people join the Roman Catholic Church. The Roman Catholic Church teaches that during the baptism, the person who is being baptized becomes free of their original sin (the sin that is passed on to each person at birth).

Kateri was given a new name after she was baptized. She was given the name Catherine. She was named after Catherine of Siena who was a mystic (a person who can communicate to the spirit world) from Italy, a country in Europe. Despite having been given a new name, she was and still is known as Kateri instead of Catherine.

St. Catherine of Siena

Kateri Goes to the Saint Francis Xavier Mission

The people in Kateri's village did not like it that she had decided to become Roman Catholic. In fact, they were so upset that some people threw rocks at her. They also said that they would keep on hurting her very much. Because she was treated so badly, Kateri decided to flee from her village.

Father de Lamberville helped Kateri and other Mohawk people who had converted (changed from one religion to another) to Roman Catholicism, to leave the village.

Father de Lamberville helped Kateri leave the village.

Kahnawake reserve is on the south shore of the St. Lawrence River in Quebec, Canada, across from Montreal.

They went to Saint Francis Xavier Mission. This mission was located 320 kilometres away from the village. It was in Sault Saint-Louis, a place not too far from Montreal, the largest city in the province of Quebec. The place is now the Kahnawake reserve.

Did you know?

A reserve is an area of land that is for the exclusive (only) use of Indigenous peoples. Many Indigenous peoples live on reserves throughout Canada.

After Kateri settled into life at Saint Francis Xavier Mission, she became a member of the Christian Iroquois women's group or Haudenosaunee. This group of women followed a lifestyle in which they chose never to get married or to engage in intimate (very close) physical activities with another person. They also practised mortification (having the strong will that is necessary in order to not give into desires of the body).

Saint Francis Xavier
Mission in the Mohawk
community of Kahnawake

Kateri learned how to control her feelings and to follow a lifestyle that she believed was right. She was pious (very religious) and this was shown by her deep faith in God and how often she prayed. The people who were around her thought that she was very kind. As a result of all this, they gave her the affectionate (showing love or kindness) name, Lily of the Mohawks.

Kateri's dedication to her faith and lifestyle did not go unnoticed. Her confessor (the priest to whom people tell their sins), Father Pierre Cholenec, reported that of all the Iroquois women who were practising the Roman Catholic faith, she was the most fervent (doing something with all one's might).

The Jesuit missionaries noticed that Kateri was able to obey all the rules that she set out to keep. Therefore, on March 25th, 1679, during the Feast of the Annunciation, Kateri was given permission by the Jesuits to take a vow (official promise) of chastity. Her vow of chastity meant that she would promise to never get married or participate in intimate physical activities with anybody.

Did you know?

The Feast of the Annunciation is when the Roman Catholic Church remembers the time when the angel Gabriel came to the Virgin Mary to tell her that she was going to become the mother of Jesus Christ, the Son of God. This feast is celebrated annually (once every year) on March 25th.

Kateri was given permission by the Jesuits to take a vow of chastity.

The vow of chastity was not difficult for Kateri, because she always had this way of thinking. In fact, even before she left her Mohawk village, she had already refused to get married a few times. It was not common for a young woman to refuse a marriage proposal because people were expected to get married.

The Death of Kateri

During the time that Kateri lived, there were different epidemics and wars. These two things made life very difficult for people. Because Kateri was a person who did not usually have good health, she became quite sick.

Nevertheless, even when she was very sick, Kateri continued to be a very calm and mild person. She did not get upset even when it looked like she might not get better.

Some time later, while Kateri was on her deathbed, she received visits from a young Jesuit by the name of Claude Chauchetière. He was impressed by her positive attitude even during the period when her poor health was taking her life.

Claude Chauchetière visited Kateri while she was on her deathbed.

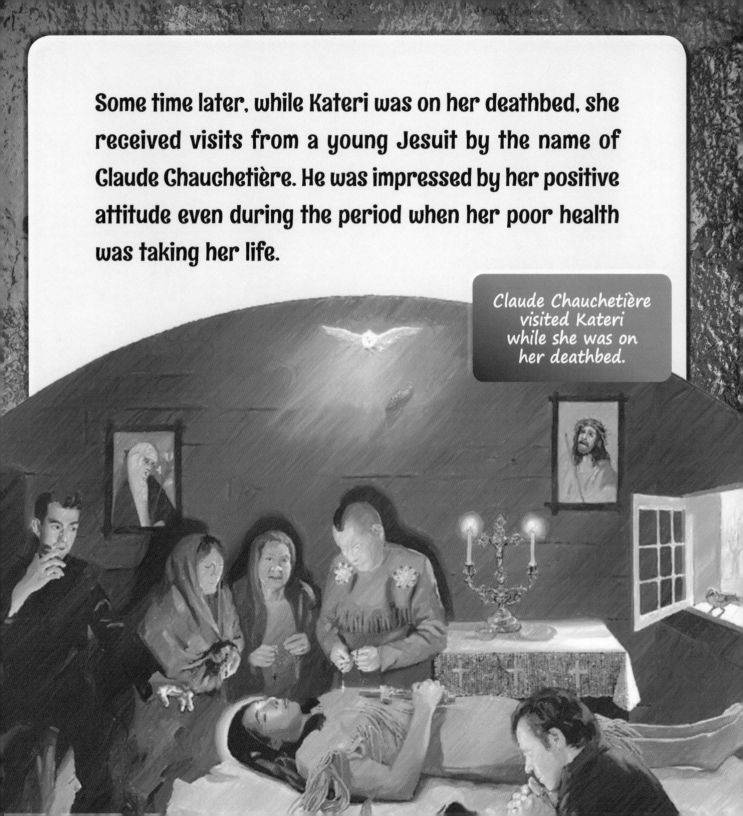

Kateri's sickness lasted a long time until one day, April 17th, 1680, she passed away. Her remains are buried at the Saint Francis Xavier Mission in Kahnawake, her place of death.

KAIATANORON
KATERI TEKAKWITHA
1656 · 1680

Kateri's remains are buried at the Saint Francis Xavier Mission in Kahnawake.

The Legacy of Kateri

In 1681, a Roman Catholic priest by the name of Father Chauchetière painted a portrait of Kateri. He also wrote a biography (a story of a person's life) of Kateri.

Kateri had another biography written about her. It was written in 1696 by a different Roman Catholic priest who was named Father Cholenec. According to the biography, the scars which had covered Kateri's body since the time when she had smallpox, disappeared fifteen minutes after she died. Then, her face took on a whiteness and radiated (lit up) with a refined beauty. The Jesuit missionaries who witnessed this event called it a miracle. It was the beginning of the legend of Kateri.

One of the oldest portraits of Kateri by Father Claude Chauchetière around 1696

Father Jacques de Lamberville had already started the work that needed to be done for Kateri's beatification. Other people added writings as well. All these people wrote documents that told details about how Kateri was able to keep a strict religious lifestyle.

An image depicting Kateri Tekakwitha

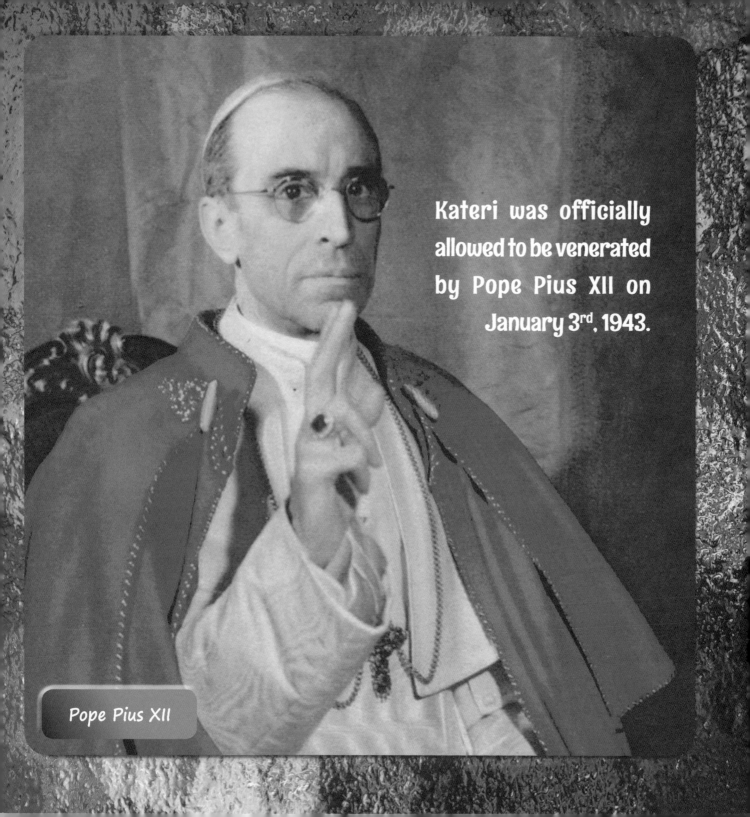

Kateri was officially allowed to be venerated by Pope Pius XII on January 3rd, 1943.

Pope Pius XII

Kateri's beatification was made official on June 22nd, 1980 by Pope John Paul II. Now, her veneration could be done so in public.

Did you know?

Beatification happens when the Pope (the leader of the Roman Catholic Church) officially states that a person who has died is in a state of complete happiness and joy. Beatification means that the dead person can be venerated (treated with great respect and awe) in public. Beatification means that the dead person may receive prayers of people on Earth and intercede (speak on behalf of someone else) to God for them. Beatification also means that at some future time, the person can be canonized (when a dead person is officially declared a saint) by the Roman Catholic Church.

Pope John Paul II

The Roman Catholic Church celebrates Kateri's feast day on July 14.

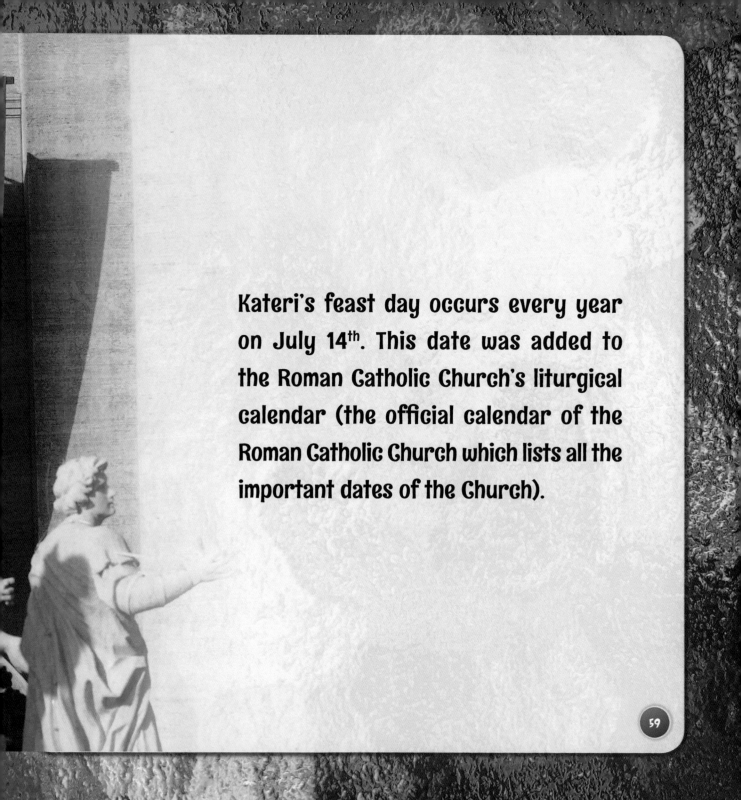

Kateri's feast day occurs every year on July 14th. This date was added to the Roman Catholic Church's liturgical calendar (the official calendar of the Roman Catholic Church which lists all the important dates of the Church).

Later, on October 21st, 2012, Kateri was canonized by Pope Benedict XVI. She was the first North American Indigenous person to be canonized. Pope Benedict XVI claimed that she was responsible for the miracle that caused an eleven-year-old boy to get better after he had been suffering from necrotizing fasciitis (flesh-eating bacteria). This happened in 2006.

Kateri was canonized by Pope Benedict XVI at the Vatican in Rome, Italy, on October 21, 2012.

A St. Kateri Tekawitha statue at St. Mary's Basilica in Phoenix, Arizona

Kateri has been called the Patroness or Patron saint of Indigenous people and of Ecology (the study of how organisms (living things) get along with other organisms and their environment) and the environment itself. Some people pray to her when they become sick.

Two churches have been named in honour of Kateri. Both of these churches are in Quebec. One church is in Uashat Mak Maliotenam and the other is in Mashteuiatsh. Both of these places are Innu communities.

Did you know?

The Innu are Indigenous people from the northeast of the province of Quebec and some eastern parts of Labrador (a part of the province of Newfoundland and Labrador, Canada's most eastern province). The Innu call this area Nitassinan, which means *our land* in English.

Kateri Tekakwita Church in Mashteuiatsh, Québec, Canada

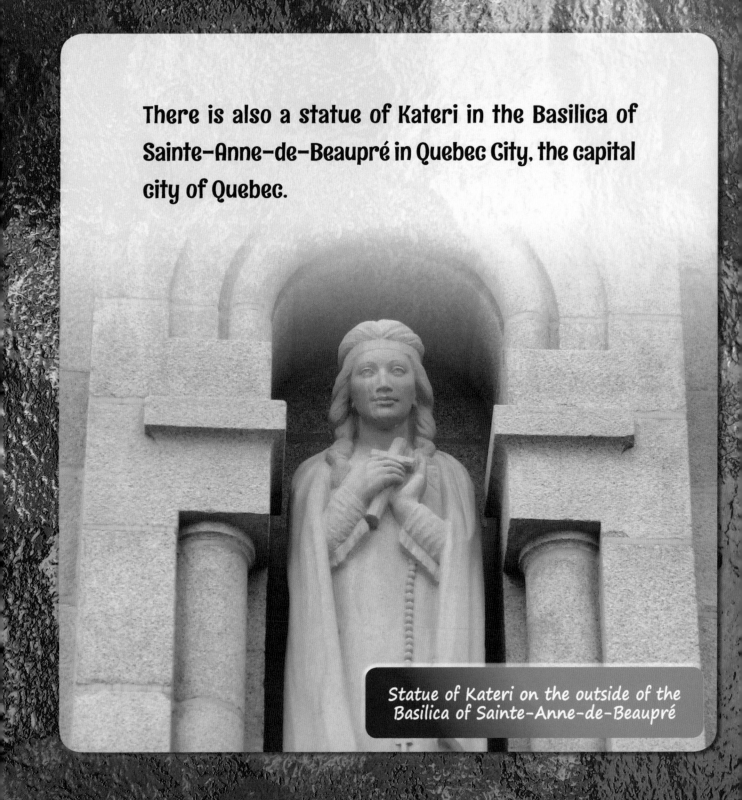

There is also a statue of Kateri in the Basilica of Sainte-Anne-de-Beaupré in Quebec City, the capital city of Quebec.

Statue of Kateri on the outside of the Basilica of Sainte-Anne-de-Beaupré

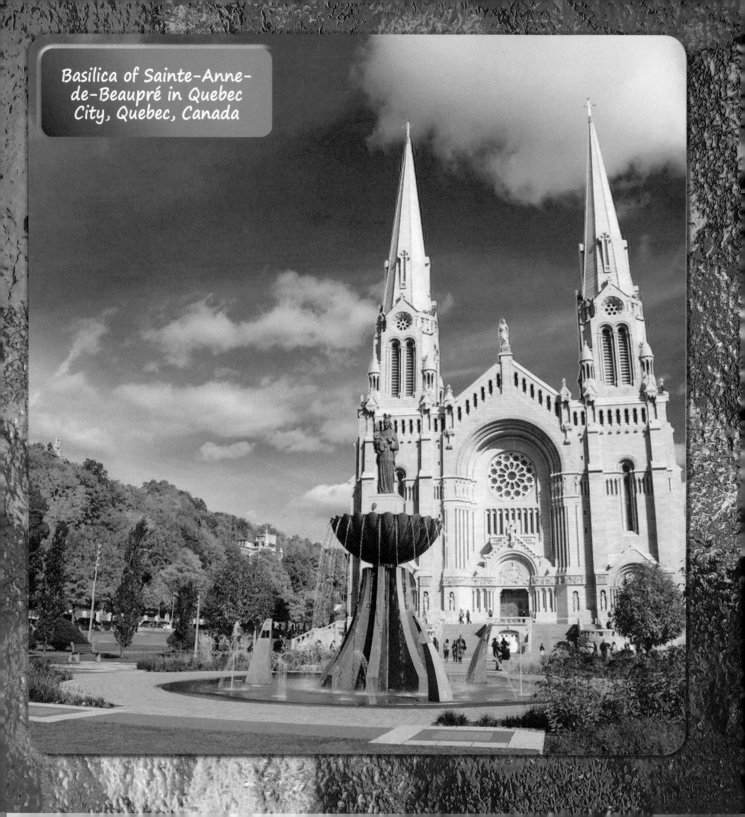

Basilica of Sainte-Anne-de-Beaupré in Quebec City, Quebec, Canada

Although some people claim that Kateri was a person who was negatively influenced by European colonists (people who come to a land and control the people who had already been living there), she is considered to be a true Canadian hero.

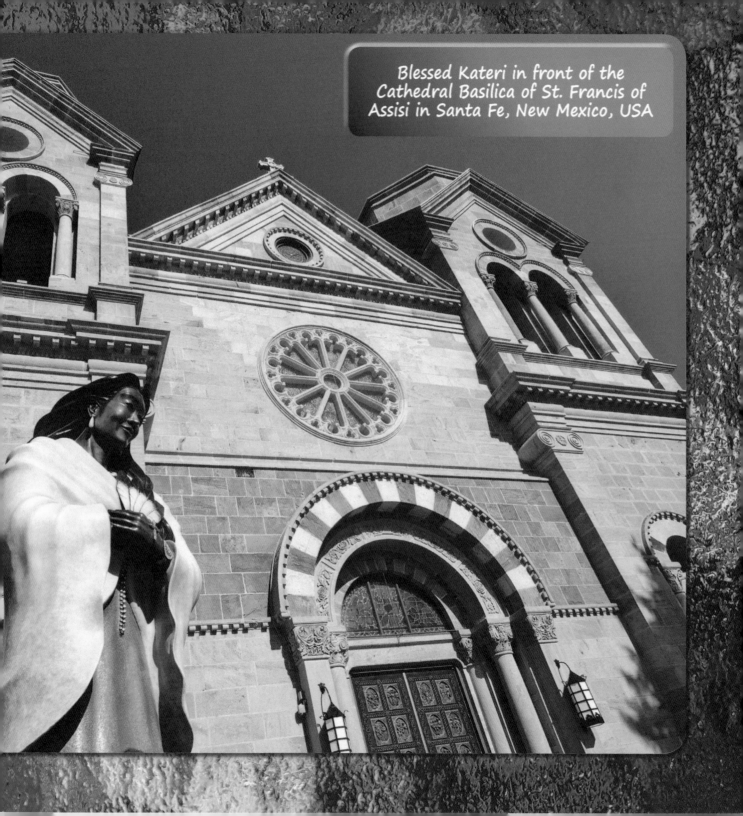

Blessed Kateri in front of the Cathedral Basilica of St. Francis of Assisi in Santa Fe, New Mexico, USA

Visit

www.truecanadians.ca

TRUE

CANADIAN SERIES

to learn about other True Canadian
stories and/or view our catalogue of
edutaining children's books.

Printed in Great Britain
by Amazon

16465433R00042